The Human Dog Sled Race

This is a work of fiction. Names, characters, places, and incidents either are the product of the author's imagination or are used fictitiously. Any resemblance to actual persons, living or dead, events, or locales is entirely coincidental.

First paperback edition November 2024

Book design by Mehgan Ducharme

Illustrations by Mehgan Ducharme

ISBN 978-1-0690697-0-2 (paperback)

ISBN 978-1-0690697-1-9 (ebook)

To my nephews, Daxton, Keaton, and Noah -
Thanks for always joining me on my crazy adventures.

In a small Northern Manitoba town, lived three boys – Daxton, Keaton, and Noah.

WELCOME
TO
THE PAS

The human dog sled race was only a few days away! They were hard at work building their dog sled.

They had to look at the rules one more time to ensure they followed them perfectly.

Finally, their dog sled was finished! The human dog sled race was now only two days away!

Human Dog Sled Race Rules:

1. No real sleds can be used
2. Minimum 4 racers, Maximum 6 racers
3. Teams must have 2 adults and up to 4 kids racing
4. Sleds must be made from recycled materials
5. Prizes for 1st, 2nd, 3rd and Most Creative Sled

Date: February 15 @ 12:00pm

Devon Park

That night Daxton, Keaton, and Noah went to bed with huge smiles on their faces.

They had magnificent dreams of winning the race and most creative sled too!

Throughout the night, a massive snowstorm rolled through town! It brought mountains of snow and harsh winds!

When the boys woke in the morning, they went to check on their dog sled, but they couldn't find it!

It was buried under a mountain of snow! Oh no! The big race was only a day away. What were they going to do?

They dug and dug until they got their dog sled free, only to discover the wind blew holes through it and made a few dents too.

The boys were feeling upset and defeated, so their parents sat them down to try and find a way to fix the dog sled.

They started by getting their extra materials out and trying to patch up their sled.

With the new patches the sled just wasn't the same, and the dents would not come out. They had no idea what to do.

Daxton, Keaton, and Noah went to bed in hopes a fresh mind would give them new ideas.

The next day, Daxton had an idea. He asked his dad if he could use one of his tarps.

They got a small tarp and decided this would be their new dog sled, but how was Noah supposed to stay on it?

Keaton had the idea to fold the tarp in half and tie it together on two sides.

Noah thought it needed some layers for comfort and put blankets and pillows in the bottom.

The boys rushed to the race and got into position with their dads at the starting line.

START

The race began! They zigged, and they zagged all the way to the finish line.

FINISH

Daxton, Keaton, Noah, and their dads won first place and most creative sled!

#1
MOST
CREATIVE
SLED

www.ingramcontent.com/pod-product-compliance
Lightning Source LLC
LaVergne TN
LVHW071226160826
845679LV00003B/914
9781069069702